An Edu...

PORTRAITS OF
QUEEN
ELIZABETH I

CLARE GITTINGS

Education Officer, National Portrait Gallery

Six Posters • 32-Page Booklet

NATIONAL PORTRAIT GALLERY

in association with the

NATIONAL MARITIME MUSEUM

Published in Great Britain by National Portrait Gallery Publications,
National Portrait Gallery,
St Martin's Place,
London WC2H 0HE

in association with the

National Maritime Museum
Greenwich
London SE10 9NF

to accompany the exhibition
ELIZABETH
at the National Maritime Museum
1 May – 14 September 2003
Sponsored by Morgan Stanley

For a complete catalogue of current publications,
please write to the National Portrait Gallery,
or visit our website at www.npg.org.uk/publications

Copyright © 2003 National Portrait Gallery

The moral right of the author has been asserted. All rights reserved. No part of this publication may be reproduced, stored in a retrieval system, or transmitted by any other means, whether electronic or mechanical, including photocopying, recording or otherwise, without the prior permission in writing of the publisher.

ISBN 1 85514 520 0

A catalogue record for this pack is available from the British Library

Text: Clare Gittings
Consultants: Tarnya Cooper, Michelle Ruddenklau and Rosalind Farrell
Senior Editor: Anjali Bulley
Design: Ivo Marloh
Production: Ruth Müller-Wirth
Illustrations (pp.16 and 27): Susie Foster
Printed in England

OUTSIDE FRONT COVER: Elizabeth I by an unknown artist (NPG 5175)

INSIDE FRONT COVER: Elizabeth I by Nicholas Hilliard, 1572,
Miniature on vellum, 51 x 48mm (NPG 108)

INSIDE BACK COVER: Elizabeth I when Princess, by an unknown artist, formerly attributed to William Scrots (fl.1537–53)
Oil on panel, 1089 x 816 mm
The Royal Collection © 2002, Her Majesty Queen Elizabeth II

OUTSIDE BACK COVER: Elizabeth I by John Bettes the Younger, c.1570
Oil on panel, 1195 x 915mm
Courtesy of the National Maritime Museum, London

CONTENTS

Introduction	4
The 'Coronation' portrait	9
The 'Phoenix' portrait	13
The 'Darnley' portrait	17
The 'Armada' portrait	21
The 'Ditchley' portrait	24
The 'Rainbow' portrait	29

POSTERS

- *The 'Coronation' portrait* by an unknown artist
- *The 'Phoenix' portrait* attributed to Nicholas Hilliard
- *The 'Darnley' portrait* by an unknown artist
- *The 'Armada' portrait* attributed to George Gower
- *The 'Ditchley' portrait* by Marcus Gheeraerts the Younger
- *The 'Rainbow' portrait* attributed to Marcus Gheeraerts the Younger

INTRODUCTION

The portraits in this pack span more than forty years of Elizabeth I's reign (1558-1603). During this time the Queen's courtiers commissioned paintings that developed both her own image and a complex set of personal symbols (for example, poster 5). These reflected, and helped to counteract, the often difficult situations in which she found herself. Her accession to the throne presented her with the traditional symbols of royalty, to which her own unique iconography was added by courtiers, officials and artists working for the court. Her gender, her unmarried state and the effects of her ageing were all addressed in the portraits.

Power, imperial claims and her relationship with her courtiers and subjects were equally prominent themes. By commissioning portraits of the Queen, her courtiers both expressed their loyalty to her and helped to develop the wide range of emblems and visual devices through which her propaganda could be promulgated. Some of her portraits reflect religious tensions during her reign, while others emphasise her wisdom. Specific moments in history, such as the attack by the Spanish Armada, as well as more personal events, such as jousts in her honour and her progresses around the country, are also referred to in Elizabeth's portraiture.

Based on the teaching practices of the National Portrait Gallery's Education Department, this resource pack shows how portraits can be used as historical sources.

Ideal for teachers working with Key Stage 2 and 3 classes, the information provided here can be adapted for both older and younger pupils. It has particular relevance to:

- Key Stage 2 Tudor History

- Key Stage 3 QCA History Study Unit 5, 'Elizabeth I: how successfully did she tackle the problems of her reign?', and Unit 7, 'Images of an age: what can we learn from portraits 1500-1750?'

- Key Stage 4 Schools History Project option on Elizabethan England

- A/S and A Level History courses.

The pack also includes suggestions for practical art, craft and design/technology projects at a range of levels, taking the portraits of Elizabeth as their starting point.

Designed for ease of use, the booklet consists of logical discussions for each of the images reproduced as posters. These notes include an introduction to each image, written at teacher-level and designed to provide background information, which should be read **before taking the session (set in italic text)**. Alongside this is a structured class discussion which provides relevant questions teachers should ask their class or group. Suggested pupil answers are **given in brackets** - it may be necessary to add extra questions to help develop discussion. Additional information which must be fed into the session is **shown in boxes**; it is clearly indicated where this information should be introduced. Suggested activities relating to each picture or topic are also included, with black-and-white photocopy masters (figs 3-9) provided to help facilitate practical exercises.

opposite page:
fig.1 **Elizabeth I**
Unknown artist, c.1560
Oil on panel, 394 x 273mm
(NPG 4449)

fig.2 **Sir Walter Ralegh** (1552?-1618)
Attributed to the monogrammist 'H', 1588
Oil on panel, 914 x 746mm
(NPG 7)

The story of Elizabeth's imagery began when she was still a princess (fig.3 and inside back cover), long before her coronation (poster 1). The Queen seems to have been reluctant on various occasions to sit to an artist. As well as presenting the new monarch to her people, there was a need for portraits as part of the negotiations for possible foreign marriages, though no surviving portrait can be linked to any of Elizabeth's specific suitors. There are very few portraits from the first decade of her reign and some of those, apparently, 'did nothing resemble [her] Majesty' (fig.1).

In the 1570s, when she was in her forties, the Queen was painted by Nicholas Hilliard, both 'in large' (poster 2 and fig.4) and in miniature (inside front cover). In all, she seems to have been painted just eight times from life. There was great demand for her image and considerable concern that unapproved portraits would circulate. To prevent this, a face pattern was produced and artists were compelled to use it or have their paintings confiscated and burnt in the royal kitchens. The face pattern, from the so-called 'Darnley' portrait (poster 3), was used to create many further 'approved' portraits (outside back cover).

In the 1580s a whole wealth of symbolism began to be used in Elizabeth's portraits. This included well-known emblems, such as the sword of justice and the olive branch of peace, and others more obscure for modern viewers. For example, ermine appears both as fur on her clothes (poster 1 and figs 8 and 9) and as a little animal. Wearing ermine was restricted to people of royal or noble blood. It symbolised purity, because an ermine would reputedly kill itself rather than live in a damaged state.

It is also from this period onwards that Elizabeth begins to appear frequently in her portraits in her favourite colours of black and white, wearing a mass of pearls (poster 4). Pearls were symbolic, through the resemblance between a pearl and the full moon. The moon was associated with chastity as the moon goddess was a virgin. Sometimes this goddess is named Cynthia, and sometimes Diana, whose symbol, the crescent moon, Elizabeth is shown wearing in her hair (poster 6). The emphasis on the Queen's virginity becomes particularly strong in her portraits after 1584, when all thoughts of marriage were finally abandoned (she was over fifty years old by then).

In his portrait of 1588 (fig.2) Walter Ralegh displays a courtier's response to Elizabeth's personal symbolism. He has dressed in black and white, encrusted with pearls, with a small crescent moon in a corner of the painting and the Latin inscription *amor et virtute* (love and virtue). As the author of a poem to Elizabeth addressing her as 'Cynthia', Ralegh played a major role in promoting the cult of the Queen as moon goddess with supernatural powers.

Victory over the Spanish Armada in 1588 was the stimulus for a further portrait of the Queen (poster 4 and fig.6). Armada imagery appears again in her famous 'Ditchley' portrait of 1592 (poster 5), where it is coupled with references to her relationship with her courtier and champion in the tiltyard, Sir Henry Lee (fig.7).

By the mid-1590s, Elizabeth's face had aged to the point where she would no longer sit for her portrait (an unfinished miniature of 1592 by Isaac Oliver marks the last time she did so). Instead, the earliest images from her youth were copied and reused in portraits such as the 'Rainbow', so that she sometimes even appears with long, flowing hair again (poster 6). The art historian Sir Roy Strong has aptly called this recycling of her younger image 'the mask of youth'. The Queen's personal symbolism reached its zenith in her final years. Even death did not halt the production of her image as James I, her successor, created a grand monument to her in Westminster Abbey (figs 8 and 9).

FURTHER READING

Roy Strong, *Gloriana: The Portraits of Elizabeth I* (Thames & Hudson, 1987)

David Starkey (guest curator); Susan Doran (ed.) *Elizabeth: The Exhibition at the National Maritime Museum* (Chatto & Windus, 2003)

ACTIVITIES

1) **Before using the portraits of Elizabeth I in this pack.** Give pupils newspaper photographs of current and recent political figures which have been taken as obviously posed 'photo opportunities'. Discuss the message each image is attempting to put across and introduce the concepts of propaganda and flattery.

2) **While using the pack.** Gradually create a timeline with the portraits, identifying major events in Elizabeth's reign as part of the sequence.

3) **After using the portraits in this pack.** An exhibition of portraits of famous Britons needs to include just one image of Elizabeth I. Debate which portrait pupils would choose to include, exploring the reasons for their choices.

4) **Portraits and other sources.** Examine a collection of coins and banknotes which feature the head of the Queen today. How does Elizabeth II appear on our money? Is she serious or smiling; does she look old or young, ugly or beautiful? What message or image of the monarch is being portrayed?

Now try to find a recent picture of Elizabeth II from a magazine or on the Internet. Most people will see the Queen regularly on television. Does she always look as she does on the coins and banknotes? Think about her clothes, her age and her expressions.

Imagine you had never seen Queen Elizabeth II before. Make a list of how many things you could learn about her just from her picture on a coin or banknote. Would you be able to make an accurate judgement of what sort of queen she is? How much would you learn about her personality?

Most people during the reign of Queen Elizabeth I would know her image only from how it appeared on coins, as portraits were largely hung within the houses of the rich. Fortunately, we still have some of her portraits from which to learn about her life and times. Select four portraits from the pack. List all the things they tell you about:

- Elizabeth's appearance
- Elizabeth's personality
- Life in Elizabethan England
- Events in Elizabeth's life.

Can you trust all of the information given in these portraits to be accurate? Now try to list what the portraits *do not tell* you about the four themes above. Suggest what other kinds of evidence an historian would need to try to find to tell him or her more.

ELIZABETH I THE 'CORONATION' PORTRAIT
By an unknown artist, c.1600

INTRODUCTION

The 26-year-old Elizabeth is shown in her coronation robes. These were woven with gold and silver thread and decorated with Tudor roses and fleurs-de-lis, this last representing the English claim to French soil. The fur lining is ermine, each black dot being the tail of one animal. Interestingly, these robes were not made specifically for Elizabeth but were reused from the coronation of her sister, Mary I, five years before, when England still held Calais.

Unlike most Tudor portraits, the Queen is shown full face. Queens were traditionally crowned with their hair loose and flowing like this. The coins and seals for the new reign were based on this image of Elizabeth. With its unattainable pose and rather blank expression but a wealth of royal symbols, it provides the starting point for the development of her portraits as queen.

fig.3 Elizabeth I when Princess, by an unknown artist, formerly attributed to William Scrots (fl.1537-53)
Oil on panel, 1089 x 816mm
The Royal Collection © 2002, Her Majesty Queen Elizabeth II

STRUCTURED DISCUSSION

What event is the picture celebrating?
(The coronation of Elizabeth I.)

How do you know she is a queen?
(Crown, orb, sceptre.)

What else makes her look regal?
(Gold clothes, ermine fur, jewels.)

What shows which country/countries she claims to rule?
(Tudor roses on dress for England and Wales; also fleurs-de-lis, staking her claim to France. Of course this was only a claim, as her sister, Mary, lost England's last French possession, Calais.)

Could she really have been this thin?
(No.)

So why has she been painted this thin?
(Flattery - it was fashionable to be thin.)

How do you think her bodice was made to push her into this shape?
(It would have had bone, steel or wooden sticks inside.)

How would this have felt?
(Extremely uncomfortable.)

What is she wearing around her neck?
(A ruff.)

What would that have done to her movements?
(Restricts turning her head.)

What is the dress fabric made of?
(Gold and silver thread, fur lining.)

How would this have felt to wear?
(Hot, heavy, hard to move.)

Do you think she would have worn clothes like this every day?
(No, these were ceremonial robes. She also had a huge number of dresses, some of which appear in other portraits, and looser gowns for when she was not in public.)

The portrait of her as a princess, formerly attributed to William Scrots, and painted in about 1547, provides a more lifelike impression of Elizabeth's face, while emphasising her learning and her devotion to religion (fig.3 and inside back cover). It also, incidentally, gives a far more realistic impression of the texture of the coronation robes, which were made of fabric similar to the front part of the skirt she wears as a princess.

The coronation image clearly dates from about 1559 but this actual painting is post-humous, based on a now lost original. The wooden panel on which it is painted has been dated to c.1600-10, using dendrochronology (counting tree rings). The gold of her robes is not painted but was created by applying layers of gold leaf to the picture surface.

It seems odd that the Queen should choose to make herself so uncomfortable. Why did she do it?
(To look grand, to be fashionable.)

Often when something is fashionable there are important messages lying behind that fashion: for example, what would happen if Elizabeth dropped a glove?
(A servant would pick it up - she could not possibly bend down herself. The clothes tell you that she does not need to move herself, as servants will wait on her.)

How does the colour of her face strike you?
(Very pale, white, possibly ill-looking.)

How did she make her face this colour?
(Powder, either made of eggshells or white lead.)

Go from the far corners of her eyebrows up to her forehead. What colour do you see?
(Bluish grey.)

What do you have in your skin that colour?
(Veins.)

If her face is covered with powder, how can you see the veins?
(Because they have been painted onto her face on top of her make-up.)

What does she want to suggest her skin is like if you can see the veins?
(See-through, transparent.)

Does all this sound beautiful to you?
(No, we tend to find it rather unpleasant.)

Again, her skin colour is giving a message about her way of life. What makes white skin tan?
(Sunlight.)

So what is she saying by being so white?
(That she does not go into the sun.)

How can she avoid the sunshine?
(By sending servants to get things for her.)

How does this compare with most of her subjects?
(Many people were involved in agriculture in Tudor England and were very tanned.)

In what position is her face?
(Fullface. This is very unusual in Tudor portraiture and was done because the coinage was made from this image.)

How is her hair done?
(Long and loose - the traditional style of hair for a Queen's coronation.)

Does her hairline look in the right place (compare hers with that of the people around you)?
(No, it is really far back on her head. Elizabethan women plucked their hairlines to make their faces look longer.)

How old does she look?
(Guesses usually between fourteen and twenty-one. She is actually twenty-six but looks younger because of her long hair.)

Is she standing up or sitting down?
(Both or neither. This is an impossible pose which is not meant to be realistic - symbolism and wealth are what matter in this portrait.)

ACTIVITIES

1) **Discussion point.** When she was twenty-three, Princess Elizabeth was described by a foreign visitor: 'Her face is comely rather than handsome, but she is tall and well formed, with good skin, although swarthy; she has fine eyes.' Which of these two portraits (fig.3 and poster 1) of the young Elizabeth, if either, does this description match more closely? Why is there a difference between what the foreigner reported and how Elizabeth appears in her portraits?

2) **Making plaster seals and jewels.** Flatten out a ball of Plasticine to make a circular tile approximately 10cm across. To make a seal, draw the coronation image of Elizabeth onto the Plasticine tile, gouging the design well into the surface. Create a retaining wall of Plasticine around the image and pour on plaster of Paris. When the plaster has hardened, remove it from the Plasticine mould and choose a colour for the seal (seals were stamped into coloured wax). Alternatively, copy one of the jewels from Elizabeth's portraits - the cross she is wearing as a princess would be ideal. Follow the same process on a lozenge-shaped Plasticine tile, placing a loop of wire at the top of the jewel before pouring in the plaster so that the jewel can then be worn on a ribbon when it has been coloured.

3) **Elizabethan beauty.** Use face paints to create the Elizabethan idea of beauty. Make the face as white as possible, redden the lips and cheeks and then draw blue veins on the temples, starting at the end of the eyebrows. The eyebrows should be concealed as far as possible (a real Elizabethan lady would have plucked hers). Take the hair back off the face to expose as much forehead as possible (again, this might have been plucked). Does a face with Elizabethan make-up look beautiful?

ELIZABETH I THE 'PHOENIX' PORTRAIT
Attributed to Nicholas Hilliard, c.1575

INTRODUCTION

This portrait takes its name from the jewel that Elizabeth is wearing just above her hand. Together with its companion portrait, the 'Pelican', it marks the beginning of Elizabeth's personal iconography in her portraiture, though neither symbol was unique to her. The pelican was believed to pierce its own breast and shed its blood to feed its young. It was therefore used in the Middle Ages as a symbol for Christ dying on the Cross to save mankind, as well as conveying the idea of charity. Although Elizabeth wears it as a symbol of her love for her people, the older religious connotations still remained.

The rose she holds in the 'Phoenix' portrait, and the rose jewel directly above the phoenix, its huge diamond surrounded by enamelled gold petals, similarly have religious, as well as dynastic, connotations. The rose was the medieval symbol of the Virgin Mary. Elizabeth's sister, Mary I, had taken the rose as her emblem, hoping to emulate her namesake's motherhood. By adopting

▷

fig.4 The 'Pelican' portrait (detail)
Attributed to Nicholas Hilliard, c.1574
Oil on panel, 787 x 610mm
Courtesy of the Walker Art Gallery, Liverpool

STRUCTURED DISCUSSION

What are the main differences between this and the Coronation portrait?
(Suggestions include the position of her face; colour and design of her clothes, not wearing a gold crown, length of her hair, colour of the background, only one hand shown here, the items she is holding, her jewels.)

What is she holding in her hand in the painting?
(A rose.)

Why has she chosen this to hold?
(It is a Tudor emblem, as well as symbolizing beauty and love - as on St Valentine's Day today. It is also a sign for the Virgin Mary.)

The Virgin Mary was the mother of Jesus. Was Elizabeth I actually anyone's mother?
(No.)

She always said that she was like a mother to a very large number of people. Who were they?
(Her subjects, the people of England.)

Where on her can you find a rose made of jewels?
(There is one in the centre of the front of her dress and one on each shoulder.)

The large black jewel in the middle of the rose on her front is a diamond. Have you ever seen a diamond this big?
(Probably not. This one was an heirloom inherited from her father, Henry VIII. Today you can see some very large diamonds in the Crown Jewels in the Tower of London.)

Describe what you can see between the rose made of diamond and her hand.
(A bird standing with large, spread wings.)

What colours are the bird and what it is standing on?
(Red and gold, and the red jewel it is standing on is a ruby.)

The bird is called a phoenix. It has very bright coloured feathers. There is only ever one phoenix at a time and it lives in the desert for over 500 years. It then burns itself to death in a fire, from the ashes of which a new phoenix is born.

the rose, Elizabeth cleverly positioned herself, the 'Virgin Queen', as the successor to the Virgin Mary, whose cult had been swept away by the Reformation in England.

The phoenix itself symbolises Elizabeth's uniqueness, there only ever being one of these mythical birds at a time. Because a new phoenix arises from the funeral pyre of its predecessor, it is a symbol of both the Resurrection and chastity. The use of religious imagery in these portraits may be in response to the excommunication of Elizabeth by the Pope in 1570 and the beginning of the Catholic plots against her centred around her cousin, Mary Queen of Scots. The virtual reversibility of the 'Phoenix' and 'Pelican' images of Elizabeth underlines the demand for multiple copies of her portraits. Both paintings are probably by Nicholas Hilliard, whose finest work is not these large-scale pictures but his miniatures. Hilliard recorded his 1572 encounter with the Queen, resulting in his first miniature of her (inside front cover), in his treatise on miniature painting, The Art of Limning. *Elizabeth chose to sit 'in the open alley of a goodly garden, where no tree was near, nor any shadows at all', believing, wrongly, that Italian painters avoided shadows in their work. Hilliard's treatise contains fascinating details of the process of miniature painting.*

▷

Does a phoenix really exist or is it a mythological (made-up) bird?
(Of course it is mythological.)

Why might wearing a phoenix show people that Elizabeth is unlike anyone else, that she is unique?
(There is only ever one phoenix at a time.)

Her brother, Edward, also used the phoenix as his special sign because his mother, Jane Seymour, had died giving birth to him. Why might a phoenix show that?
(Because one phoenix always dies before the next is born.)

What is Elizabeth holding in her hand that is outside the picture?
(Look carefully along the bottom edge of the painting.)
(A feather fan.)

Why is she holding that? (Remember that some things in her pictures are there for practical, rather than symbolic, reasons.)
(To keep cool - these clothes would be very hot to wear.)

Now look at the 'Pelican' portrait (fig.4). In what ways is it the same as the 'Phoenix' portrait?
(Same pose, same face and hair, same cut of the clothes, both have a bird jewel, same style of painting.)

In what ways are the two portraits different?
(The figure is reversed, different details on the clothes and head-dress, different jewels including a white pelican jewel in place of the phoenix, gloves instead of the rose in her hand, different feathers in her fan, different-colour backgrounds, crowned rose and fleur-de-lis in the 'Pelican' background.)

Why were two similar portraits made?
(Lots of rich people wanted portraits of the Queen and the artist, Nicholas Hilliard, was sensibly repeating his composition.)

Why aren't the two paintings just identical copies?
(Maybe people wanted to feel that they had their very own version, not one that was identical to someone else's. It was also more interesting for Hilliard to paint different details.)

When Nicholas Hilliard first painted the Queen he created a miniature portrait of her (inside front cover). Why might you want a miniature painted rather than a life-sized portrait?
(To wear as a decoration or to give as a private gift. Elizabethan miniatures are generally more valuable today than life-sized Tudor portraits.)

The skin colour, called 'carnation', was applied first. The small black dots in the pearls were originally silver, burnished with a squirrel's tooth, but have since tarnished. Hilliard also provides useful practical advice about what to do if your paint fails to adhere to your miniature: pick your ear and add the wax to your paint.

If you were Queen Elizabeth I, what would you talk to your artist about while you were being painted?
(She talked about which country had the best painters; she thought the Italians were the best artists in her day. Nowadays people having their portrait painted often discuss their favourite works of art with the artist painting them.)

If you were going to be painted by Nicholas Hilliard, would you prefer to have a miniature or a life-sized portrait, and why?
(Either, but his miniatures are actually his considered finest works.)

ACTIVITIES

1) **Miniature painting.** Choose an image from this pack to produce as either a circular or an oval miniature (although genuine miniatures are as little as 5cm high, for Key Stage 2 pupils a height of around 10cm is preferable). This activity can be made easier by 'pouncing' the outline (see Activity 1, p.19 - the face pattern in fig.5 could be reduced on a photocopier to miniature size). Work in watercolour, with a blue background as in the inside front cover, and stick sequins to the finished miniature to represent jewels. To make the activity more authentically Elizabethan, put the paint into mussel shells for pupils to use.

2) **Making clay tiles of Elizabeth I.** On a clay tile 20 to 30cm square create an image of Elizabeth I in relief based on the 'Phoenix' portrait. Mould the features of her face (clay pushed through a fine sieve makes excellent hair). Make patterns to decorate her clothes. If you are adding decoration with separate pieces of clay, stick them on firmly with very wet clay (called slip). Dry the finished relief slowly, fire in a kiln and then glaze and fire again.

fig.5 Modern face pattern based on the 'Darnley' portrait

ELIZABETH I THE 'DARNLEY' PORTRAIT

By an unknown artist, c.1575

INTRODUCTION

This portrait is named after the family who previously owned it. It is one of the finest portraits of Elizabeth I and also the one most hotly debated by art historians. It has similarities to a drawing of the Queen by the Italian artist Federigo Zuccaro which shows her in a similar head-dress, carrying a feather fan. However, attempts by Sir Roy Strong to identify the painting as Zuccaro's work have not convinced other art historians. Whoever was the artist, though, this remains among the best depictions of the Queen's face to have come down to us.

This portrait certainly is not rich in the Queen's usual emblems. Apart from the crown and sceptre on the table beside her and her interestingly looped strings of pearls, the main focus for personal symbolism is the magnificent jewel hanging from Elizabeth's waist. This has a large ruby surrounded by diamonds and other stones. Above these gems is the enamelled gold figure of the Roman goddess Minerva, while below the jewels is shown Neptune, the god of the sea. Minerva has several attributes appropriate to Elizabeth. Like Elizabeth, she is a virgin, though not lacking in suitors.

STRUCTURED DISCUSSION

How does Elizabeth look different from the way she looked in the 'Coronation' portrait?
(Suggestions include the position of her face, colour and design of her clothes, not wearing a gold crown, length of her hair, the items she is holding.)

How can you tell that she is older now than she was when she was crowned?
(Her shorter hair, and also the look around her eyes and mouth.)

Guess her age from the way she looks in this portrait.
(She was about forty-two when this was painted.)

Look carefully at the faces in this and the 'Coronation' portrait. Which looks more like a real living person?
(The 'Darnley' portrait is generally thought to be one of the best likenesses of Elizabeth to have survived.)

Look at the shape of her body in each painting. Which one makes her look more three-dimensional and which one makes her look more two-dimensional (flat)?
(The 'Coronation' portrait is more two-dimensional, with less sense of volume.)

Where are the crown and sceptre in the 'Darnley' portrait?
(On the table behind her.)

Why has the artist put them there, do you think?
(To remind viewers that Elizabeth is the Queen. However, she doesn't actually have the crown on her head as she is wearing a dress, not her robes.)

What pieces of jewellery is she wearing?
(Pearls as a looped necklace, in her hair and round her waist; jewel with a ruby and enamelled figures hanging on a ribbon from her waist.)

Is this how we would wear jewellery today?
(We would be unlikely to loop a necklace like this or to hang something very valuable from the waist.)

The little figure standing on top of her ruby is the Roman goddess of peace and wisdom, called Minerva. What is Elizabeth saying about herself by wearing this jewel?
(Both that she is very rich, to be able to afford such a jewel, and that she is peaceful and wise, like Minerva.)

She wears a helmet and carries a spear and shield ready for war, but is primarily renowned for her peacefulness and, above all, her wisdom. In a contest between Minerva and Neptune over who could provide the better gift to Athens, Minerva (called 'Athena' by the Greeks) won by creating an olive tree for the inhabitants, symbolising peace and plenty, and therefore gave her name to the city.

The 'Darnley' image is particularly important in the development of Elizabeth's portraiture because the face pattern based on it was used most frequently to produce further portraits of the Queen (the technique for doing this is described in Activity 1 below). Portraits made from the 'Darnley' face pattern appear throughout the 1570s, 1580s and even the early 1590s. They show Elizabeth facing in either direction and were employed by a range of artists with varying levels of skill. Six are attributed to John Bettes the Younger and show the Queen with a variety of different accessories, including a fan, gloves, a sceptre (outside back cover) and, more incongruously, a sieve. In part, this symbolised her discernment in sifting good from bad. It also referred to her chastity, as the Vestal Virgins in Rome were reputedly so pure they could carry water from the River Tiber in a sieve (apparently they achieved this by first rubbing mutton fat into the mesh of the sieve to seal the holes).

How does the bodice (jacket) she is wearing do up?
(You can see buttons down the front, with red decoration called 'frogging', rather like some later military uniforms. This fashion was called 'Polish' style in Elizabeth's reign.)

Her sleeves and her cuffs are made separately from the main part of her bodice. What can you see where the cuffs join the sleeves and where the sleeves meet her bodice on her shoulders?
(They are laced together with white ribbons which create decorative puffs along the joins. Before there were zips, elastic or Velcro, items of clothing needed to come into many more different pieces than they do now.)

What is the most colourful thing in the picture?
(Her fan.)

Do these feathers come from British birds?
(No, they are too exotic.)

Now look at the painting by John Bettes the Younger of Elizabeth (on the outside back cover). It was made over ten years later (the bigger ruff came into fashion during the 1580s). One important part of this picture looks similar to the 'Darnley' portrait. What is it?
(Her face, though it has been reversed by Bettes.)

Bettes never painted the Queen from life, so what did he use to paint this portrait of her?
(The 'Darnley' portrait.)

To be precise, he used a face pattern from the 'Darnley' sitting - see Activity 1 below - which is why only the face is similar and why it was easy for him to reverse the direction she is facing. He made at least six portraits of Elizabeth using this face pattern, all with slightly different clothes, jewellery, backgrounds and things she is holding. No original face patterns of Elizabeth exist today but some survive for other Tudor sitters.

There are still well over 100 portraits of Elizabeth I surviving and many more would have originally existed. Why do you think Elizabeth wanted painters to use her face pattern?
(She couldn't have sat individually for hundreds of portraits but she wanted to make sure her face looked good in all the pictures of her. If painters did not use the face pattern, then their pictures could be taken away and burnt in the royal ovens.)

Which do you think is the better painting of her, the 'Darnley' or the one by Bettes?
(The 'Darnley' is far less mechanical than Bettes's work.)

ACTIVITIES

1) **Pouncing.** Elizabeth I was extremely concerned about how she looked, particularly as she aged. She insisted that artists used her approved face pattern. Get half the class to pounce pictures of Elizabeth using the drawn face pattern (fig.5) and the other half to copy Elizabeth direct from the poster. For the pouncing activity you will need photocopies of fig.5.

   Place a sheet of tracing paper under it and prick through the lines with a darning needle or awl. (If preparing a class set, several sheets can be pricked at once.) Then place the tracing paper on a clean sheet of paper and rub charcoal or dark chalk through the holes. The pictures can then be completed in colour. Which method produces more accurate pictures of Elizabeth? Which method shows more of the artist's individuality? Which would Elizabeth have wanted? Which do we like better?

2) **Blackwork embroidery.** Copy the patterns embroidered in black thread on the white sleeves of the portrait by John Bettes (outside back cover), around the shoulders of the 'Phoenix' portrait (poster 2) and the sleeves of the 'Pelican' portrait (fig.4). Transfer one design onto white cotton fabric (perhaps by pouncing it using dressmaker's chalk - see Activity 1) and embroider the design in black thread. Blackwork was a very common form of Elizabethan decoration and appears, with different designs, in all six of Bettes's portraits of Elizabeth I.

fig. 6 The 'Armada' portrait
By George Gower, 1588, Oil on panel, 1070 x 1350mm
Woburn Abbey © Marquess of Tavistock and the Trustees of the Bedford Estates

ELIZABETH I THE 'ARMADA' PORTRAIT

Attributed to George Gower, c.1588 21

INTRODUCTION

The 'Armada' portrait is clearly linked with the famous events of 1588. It survives in three versions of the same image, two of which have suffered badly over the years. The National Portrait Gallery version, reproduced on poster 4, has been substantially cut down from its original size. Another version, which interestingly belonged to Sir Francis Drake's family and may have been commissioned by Drake himself, has been very inaccurately overpainted at a later date. The best surviving version is that at Woburn Abbey (fig.6). The artist associated with this version was George Gower, Serjeant Painter to the Queen, a post which involved being responsible for decorative projects such as banners and palace interiors rather than the production of the Queen's likeness. He may also have been involved with the National Portrait Gallery version, although this is less clear. The Drake version may even be of a somewhat later date.

Behind the Queen are two scenes, one of the English fleet unleashing fire ships at the start of the battle and,

STRUCTURED DISCUSSION

What can you see in the background of this picture? Look carefully.
(Sea, ships.)

How is the left side of the background different from the right side?
(Ships sailing on left and sunk on right - the latter is very hard to see.)

What important event in Elizabeth's reign does this refer to?
(Spanish Armada.)

Why did Elizabeth have this portrait painted, do you think?
(To celebrate England's victory.)

Was she really painted standing by the sea while the battle took place?
(No, definitely not. It is an imaginary picture of the battle.)

Look carefully around the edges of the painting. Was the portrait actually this size when it was first made? Give your reasons.
(No, the artist would not have cut through Elizabeth's arms and hands like this.)

Why do you think it might have been cut down?
(Given the inelegant composition that resulted, it was probably done to save the picture from an attack of woodworm or rot, cutting away the infected parts to preserve the middle.)

This painting has lost a lot on both sides. What would you have put into these missing parts if you had been the artist?
(Anything suitable to the theme of the Armada: Sir Francis Drake, etc.)

Now compare the damaged painting with the complete image in fig.6. What is missing in the version on the poster?
(The crown beside the Queen on the table, her hand on a globe, the fan and the very odd-looking chair, with a mermaid-like design, which is shown simultaneously from the front and the side.)

What might she be saying by placing her hand on the globe like this?
(Claiming power greater than merely ruling England.)

Why is the chair decorated with this particular carved figure?
(The mermaid symbolises the importance of England's involvement with the sea.)

In what way does the shape of the complete 'Armada' portrait differ from the other portraits of the Queen in this pack?
(It is landscape rather than portrait, wider than it is high.)

later, the wreck of the Spanish ships in a storm. Besides her obvious wealth, Elizabeth makes claims to authority beyond that of merely ruling England. Her hand on the globe suggests a bid for a wider worldly power, while the closed, arched crown has imperial connotations.

This is, however, very much an English picture, rich with surface pattern but with no pretensions to perspective, particularly in the rendering of the chair. With its two simultaneous scenes of different moments in the battle, the painting lacks any sense of realism, but it is a fine example of Elizabethan portraiture.

Look at Elizabeth's clothes in the 'Phoenix', 'Darnley' and 'Armada' portraits. How has their shape altered from the 1570s to the 1580s?
(They become larger, changing from tighter sleeves and a more cone-shaped skirt in the 'Phoenix' and the 'Darnley' portraits to a wider skirt, supported by a farthingale, and big farthingale sleeves in the 'Armada' portraits.)

In the 'Armada' portrait what are Elizabeth's favourite colours?
(Black and white.)

What is her favourite type of jewel?
(Pearls.)

Explain how her favourite colours and jewel tell us that she was sometimes called the 'Moon Goddess'.
(Black for night, white for the moon; a pearl is like a miniature full moon.)

Are there any other references to astronomy in this picture?
(Yes, gold suns on her dress.)

Are there any references to the weather in the picture?
(Yes, the Spanish ships have been sunk by a storm. The picture hints at the idea that Elizabeth controls the weather, a theme also found in other paintings of her.)

Where is her largest pearl?
(At the bottom of the painting, over her private parts.)

What is the meaning of this?
(Her greatest pearl is her chastity. This links with the idea of the moon goddess, who was renowned for her chastity.)

ACTIVITIES

1) **Discussion point.** Elizabeth gave a famous speech to her troops when they were lined up at Tilbury, ready to fight the Spanish army if the Armada succeeded in landing in England. She included these words:
'I am resolved in the midst and heat of battle to live and die amongst you all ....
I know I have the body of a weak and feeble woman, but I have the heart and stomach of a king, and a king of England too, and think foul scorn that ... Spain, or any prince of Europe, should dare to invade the borders of my realm'.

Compare her speech with the 'Armada' portrait of Elizabeth. Do both give the same message about the Queen?

2) **Before and after.** The 'Armada' portrait includes 'before' and 'after' scenes of the famous sea battle. Describe or draw some more 'before' and 'after' scenes for other important moments in Elizabeth's reign (for example, the trial and execution of Mary, Queen of Scots).

fig.7 Sir Henry Lee (1533-1611)
By Antonis Mor, 1568
Oil on panel, 641 x 533mm
(NPG 2095)

ELIZABETH I THE 'DITCHLEY' PORTRAIT

By Marcus Gheeraerts the Younger, c.1592

INTRODUCTION

The French ambassador, writing a few years after this portrait was painted, said of Elizabeth, 'As for her face, it is and appears to be very aged. It is long and thin, and her teeth are very yellow and many of them are missing. Her figure is fair and tall and graceful whatever she does.' The artist Marcus Gheeraerts the Younger has balanced flattery with realism to produce this image of the ageing Queen. Gheeraerts himself was a foreigner, the son of a Protestant painter, and he came with his father to England to escape from the religious troubles in mainland Europe. Unlike the earlier portraits of Elizabeth, this was painted on canvas, which allowed Gheeraerts to produce a huge full-length image of the Queen.

The picture is filled with symbolism. Elizabeth's white dress reflects her virginity, while the rose pinned to her ruff represents beauty and the House of Tudor. The map of England beneath her feet displays her domination over her kingdom; standing on the globe suggests her aspiration

STRUCTURED DISCUSSION

⊙ FOCUS ON HER FACE

How old do you think the Queen is?
(She is actually fifty-nine, but people often guess that she is much younger than this.)

How has the painter made her seem younger?
(Hair colour, lack of wrinkles.)

Are there any signs of ageing?
(Bags under the eyes, a few fine lines.)

Why might she have wanted to look younger than she really was?
(Personal vanity; political reasons - she controls her court through the fiction that her courtiers are all in love with her; dangerous to appear old and weak as this might have encouraged challenges from younger claimants to the throne.)

Why is her hair this colour?
(It is a wig.)

What is odd about her mouth and why?
(It is very small, as she has lost many of her teeth.)

⊙ FOCUS ON THE BACKGROUND

What is under her feet?
(A map of England.)

Why?
(She rules it.)

What is the map on?
(A globe.)

Why?
(She is claiming imperial powers; it refers to her status as a ruler.)

What can you see in the sea?
(Ships and sea monsters.)

Why might they be there?
(Possible reference to the Armada, or to exploration; also a conventional map decoration at that time.)

Describe the weather in this picture.
(Storms to the right, sunshine to the left.)

Which way is Elizabeth facing?
(Towards the sunny side.)

to imperial power. The strange mixture of weather - storms and sunshine - conveys the fact that she has successfully brought her country through troubled times to its present happy state. The storm also recalls the destruction of the Spanish Armada, as do the English ships around the coastline.

As well as these political symbols, the picture has a personal message too: the portrait commemorates Elizabeth's forgiveness of one of her courtiers, Sir Henry Lee (fig.7), for having taken a mistress. It is on Lee's house at Ditchley in Oxfordshire that she is standing on the map and this is what gives the portrait its usual title.

Elizabeth is standing on Ditchley, the house of her courtier Sir Henry Lee. This picture, known as the 'Ditchley' portrait, was painted for Sir Henry Lee, the Queen's champion from 1559 to 1590, and commemorates Elizabeth's visit to Lee's house at Ditchley near Oxford in September 1592. Henry had incurred Elizabeth's anger by taking a mistress, Anne Vavasour. The Queen's visit to Ditchley in 1592 was a sign that she had forgiven him for his love of Anne.

What might the weather be saying about her reign?
(That she has brought her country through difficult times - such as the Armada - to its present happy state.)

⊙ FOCUS ON THE PAINTING ITSELF

What is this portrait painted on?
(On canvas using oil paint.)

Are you seeing the whole portrait as it was originally painted?
(No, the edges have been cut down. This is especially clear along the right edge, where part of the writing is missing.)

Why might this have been done?
(To fit the portrait into a smaller space.)

⊙ FOCUS ON HER BODY AND CLOTHES

Is there any other obvious sign of flattery in this portrait?
(The waist is unnaturally thin.)

What is the significance of the colour of her dress? For younger pupils you might ask: when are long white dresses worn today?
(It conveys the idea of virginity/purity - like a wedding dress. You might then consider who or what she is married to - the country under her feet.)

What has been used to decorate her dress?
(Pearls, gold, jewels. A dress like this would be extremely costly - around £500,000 at today's prices.)

What has she got pinned to her ruff and why?
(A pink rose, which is a symbol of beauty and of the house of Tudor.)

What is she holding in her hands?
(Fan in her right hand; gloves in her left.)

Can you link these with the weather in the picture?
(Fan for sunny weather, gloves for stormy weather.)

Would it be comfortable to wear a dress like this?
(No. She is wearing her 'best' clothes for a portrait, as we might do today for a photograph. The Queen often wore a looser robe, more like a dressing gown.)

Why is Elizabeth's skirt this shape?
(There is a farthingale underneath it, symbolising wide hips for child-bearing.)

Is this the same shape as her skirt in the 'Armada' portrait?
(No, this one is called a 'wheel' farthingale.)

If you met her in this dress, would you be able to see her feet?
(No.)

Why has the painter shown her feet in this portrait?
Clue: think what she is standing on.
(To show her at a particular place on the map.)

Can you interpret the weather in this portrait in the light of the Queen's displeasure with Lee over Anne Vavasour and her subsequent forgiveness of him?
(Storms for the quarrel, sunshine for forgiveness.)

Look at the portrait of Sir Henry Lee (fig.7). On his sleeve he has a design of lover's knots and armillary spheres (circular, with a diagonal line across it). Elizabeth also wears an armillary sphere on the top half of her body. Where is it?
(Hanging below her ear. The armillary sphere was another of Elizabeth's personal emblems. In real life it was much bigger than this and was a scientific instrument used by astronomers, which led to symbolising heavenly wisdom.)

ACTIVITIES

1) Discussion point. How closely does the 'Ditchley' portrait of Elizabeth match the French ambassador's description of her, quoted in the introduction (p.24)?

2) Making a wheel farthingale. Divide pupils into groups of three or four. The farthingale needs to be made on one pupil, who acts as a model, with two or three others doing the actual making. First decide whether to use fabric throughout or brown paper instead. The materials needed are cane, Rufflette (gathered curtain) tape, brown paper or buckram, old tights, newspaper or rags for stuffing, scissors, a stapler, masking tape, and more brown paper or a gathered skirt.

Start by making a 'bum roll' (the genuine Elizabethan name) by stuffing balls of newspaper (or rags) into a pair of old tights, knotting the waist and leaving the feet empty to tie round the model's waist, a bit like a rubber ring for swimming. Make a cane circle larger than the model's hips, as in the 'Ditchley' portrait of Elizabeth I. Cut three more pieces of cane the same length (cut a diagonal at one end for ease of threading).

Lightly join the ends of one cane circle with masking tape, draw round it on brown paper (or buckram) and then undo the cane again. Cut out the circle. Fold the circle in quarters and cut out the middle to fit round the model's waist. Cut from the middle of the circle to the edge. Stick the cane round the outer edge of the circle with masking tape. Put the circle on to the model, on top of the bum roll, and stick the ends of the cane together again.

Cut a length of Rufflette tape and tie it in a bow around the model's waist to form a waistband. Staple one end of a new length of tape to the waistband, drape this tape over the edge of cane ring and drop to it the floor, cutting it off at floor level. Repeat this seven more times, spacing the tape evenly around the waistband. Stick the tapes down firmly with masking tape where they pass over the edge of the cane ring.

Count down ten holes from the cane ring on each tape and mark. Thread a length of cane through all the holes at that level and join the ends of the cane with masking tape. Count down another ten holes from there and mark. Thread through another cane and join ends. Repeat for the third cane (or more, if wanted).

Cover the farthingale with either a very gathered long skirt or sheets of brown paper stuck on with masking tape (if the brown paper option is chosen, remember that the model will not be able to manage stairs).

fig.8 Electrotype of Elizabeth I's effigy in Westminster Abbey
After Maximilian Colte, c.1605–7, 965mm high
(NPG 357)

ELIZABETH I THE 'RAINBOW' PORTRAIT
Attributed to Marcus Gheeraerts the Younger, c.1600

INTRODUCTION

This is the last great portrait of Elizabeth. In it her personal symbolism reaches its apogee, creating an image of her far removed from the reality of her final years. The portrait likens her to the moon and also to the sun that creates the rainbow. The design of eyes and ears on her golden cloak celebrates both her fame and her knowledge of everything that happens in her realm. The jewelled gauntlet on her ruff refers to the jousts held in her honour.

Themes from earlier portraits reappear here. Her wisdom is shown by the jewelled serpent on her left arm, here with the added implication that her head rules her heart; a heart is shown dangling from the snake's mouth. Despite her seventy years, the spring flowers on her bodice denote youth and revitalisation. This theme is even more strikingly conveyed by the young appearance of her face. This is, of course, taken from a much earlier face pattern and bore no relation to the actual looks of the ageing Queen.

This portrait has hung at Hatfield House for all, or nearly all, of its existence. Art historians are unsure who painted it. Sir Roy Strong has suggested ▷

STRUCTURED DISCUSSION

This portrait is named after the rainbow in Elizabeth's right hand. As in the biblical story of Noah's ark, the rainbow is a sign from God. The Latin words above mean 'no rainbow without the sun'. Unfortunately, the paint has thinned over the years and so the rainbow has become transparent and lost its original colours.

Where is the 'sun' in this portrait?
(Elizabeth is the sun that makes the rainbow, which is why her cloak is this golden colour.)

There is also a crescent moon in her headdress. Can you find it?
(It is right at the top, set with diamonds, near the four big pearls in front of the feathers.)

Look at Elizabeth's face and compare it with earlier portraits of her. Which is it most like?
(It looks very young, almost as in the 'Coronation' portrait and certainly considerably younger than the 'Darnley'.)

Which was the last portrait in which she had long hair?
(The 'Coronation' portrait.)

She was actually nearly seventy years old when this portrait was painted, so how has it been made?
(Not from life but by copying an earlier portrait of her.)

Why do you think she wanted her portrait to be made this way?
(She didn't like how she looked in old age and didn't want an artist to paint her like this.)

Is she wearing a farthingale, as she was in the 'Ditchley' portrait?
(No, what she is wearing is similar to costumes worn in masques, the theatrical shows in which all the performers were courtiers.)

How many ruffs is she wearing here?
(Two, an open one, as in the 'Ditchley' portrait and a closed one around her neck, rather like in the 'Phoenix' portrait.)

Pinned on her open ruff, to the right of her face, is a piece of jewellery. What does it show?
(A gauntlet, for jousting. Sir Henry Lee (fig.7) had been the Queen's Champion and jousted in the tournament held each year to mark the day of her accession to the throne.)

Marcus Gheeraerts the Younger, painter of the 'Ditchley' portrait, but other art historians are less certain. Like the 'Darnley' portrait, its painter remains a mystery.

In direct contrast to the 'Rainbow' portrait is the posthumous image of Elizabeth by the sculptor Maximilian Colte, paid for by her successor, James I. James commissioned two monuments in Westminster Abbey, one for Elizabeth (figs 8 and 9) and one for his mother, Mary, Queen of Scots, who was Elizabeth's cousin. On her monument, Elizabeth looks her true age at death, perhaps deliberately to contrast with the idealised beauty of the younger Mary, Queen of Scots. The engraving of Elizabeth's tomb was very widely disseminated and would have been seen by many more people than saw her painted portraits (fig.9).

James was keen to emphasise the legality of his title to the English throne, so Elizabeth is shown at her most regal, crowned, with orb and sceptre, wearing her parliamentary robes, originally of red velvet and ermine. However, James also ensured that his mother's monument was taller than that of Elizabeth, who had, of course, been responsible for Mary's execution more than fifteen years before.

Are the two 'wings' behind her similar to the 'wings' she wore in the 'Ditchley' portrait?
(They are even bigger here.)

Her orange cloak has a very strange pattern on it. What can you see?
(Eyes and ears. The things that look a bit like mouths are actually folds in the material.)

What do the eyes and ears mean?
(She is so famous that she is seen and heard everywhere; also that she is very well informed and sees and hears everything that happens in her kingdom.)

On the front of her bodice (where the knot is in her rope of pearls) what decorations can you see?
(Spring flowers – pansies, honeysuckle, gillyflowers and cowslips.)

Why spring flowers?
(To suggest that she is still young, fit and beautiful.)

What has she got on the sleeve of her left arm?
(A snake made of jewels. Serpents were a symbol of wisdom and were one of the signs of the goddess Minerva – see the jewel hanging from Elizabeth's waist in poster 3.)

What does the serpent have dangling from its mouth?
(A heart.)

What is Elizabeth saying about wisdom (the snake) and love (the heart)? Which is shown as stronger here?
(The snake is holding the heart, so her wisdom controls her feelings.)

Can you recognise something from the 'Ditchley' portrait just above the serpent's head?
(An armillary sphere – see Elizabeth's earring in poster 5 and the sleeve in fig.7.)

Compare the 'Rainbow' portrait with the image on Elizabeth's tomb (fig.8) which her successor, King James I, paid for. Which makes her look older?
(The tomb.)

Which shows more obviously that she is a Queen?
(The tomb.)

Why did James choose to show her wearing her crown and as her real age when she died?
(He wants it to be really clear that she was the rightful Queen and that he is her legitimate successor, after her death from natural causes.)

How would you like best to remember her?

fig.9 Monument of Elizabeth I in Westminster Abbey
Engraving by Willem or Magdalena de Passe for Henry Holland's
Heroulogia, 1620, of the monument by Maximilian Colte, c.1605-7
(NPG Archive)

ACTIVITIES

1) **Then and now.** In groups, draw up a list of 'modern ideas of beauty' - think about what our society regards as 'beauty' in people and how famous people create these images. What features, make-up, clothing, body shapes, hairstyles, skin colours and so on are considered beautiful today?

Then go through magazines and onto the Internet to find images of famous people your group thinks represent 'beauty' in today's society. Compare the features of these people with those represented in the portraits of Elizabeth you have discussed.

Elizabeth's portraits had to represent more than just beauty. Work in your group to cut up and separate the features of the famous people you have selected. Choose different features that you feel represent **power, beauty, wisdom, intelligence** and **wealth** (remember to consider clothing, the person's expression, objects they may be holding, as with Elizabeth's portraits) and stick them together to create a 'collage portrait' entitled *Portrait of a Monarch*. Does your portrait look beautiful? Would it have looked beautiful to an Elizabethan?

Explain to the rest of the class why your group chose the features in your collage and compare each one with how Elizabeth's portraits try to represent these themes.

2) **Portraits for today.** Imagine you are going to commission your own portrait. It should reflect your personality and an important event in your life. You need to consider the following:

• What to wear - should you be wearing fashionable clothes or try to achieve a 'dateless' look?

• How would you show the event in your life - as a picture through a window; filling the whole background; using an object in the painting?

• How would you pose - would you stand or sit, smile or look serious? Where would you place your hands?

• How would you get across your personality?

Draw a rough sketch of your portrait when you have decided these things. Now write notes around the sketch, pointing out important aspects of the portrait that tell the viewer the key messages about you that you want them to know.

Choose one of the portraits of Elizabeth from the pack and draw a rough sketch of it. Add notes in the same way as with your portrait, highlighting the key messages.

3) **Eyes and ears fabric.** Paint or print some 'eyes and ears' fabric, as worn in the 'Rainbow' portrait. Printing blocks could be made from polystyrene tiles, lino, potato halves or string glued onto card.